BACK ON
YOUR BIKE

Published in 2020 by
Laurence King Publishing Ltd
361–373 City Road
London EC1V 1LR
United Kingdom
enquiries@laurenceking.com
www.laurenceking.com

A catalogue record for this book
is available from the British Library

ISBN: 978 1 78627 925 5

Design: Alexandre Coco
Senior Editor: Melissa Mellor

Printed in Italy

Laurence King Publishing is committed
to ethical and sustainable production.
We are proud participants in
The Book Chain Project
bookchainproject.com*

For Jules, with love

BACK ON YOUR BIKE

All the stuff you
need to know to be
a cyclist again

Alan Anderson

Illustrations by David Sparshott

Laurence King Publishing

Introduction

It's been a while since you last rode a bike – or perhaps you never have – and you're feeling a little uncertain about it now, although you know that a lot of people seem to like it. If you want to ride, but aren't sure how gears work, or are concerned about the traffic, don't worry: this book is here to help.

With a real-world guide to the essentials, you'll learn how to look after your bike, and how to look after yourself. There's an introduction to bike maintenance, and simple instructions for the repairs that you may have to make. If you've never ridden before, there's a simple way to learn in these pages. And then, with a clear understanding of your rights, the rules of the road and the key techniques of riding in traffic, you'll be able to navigate the city's streets safely.

That, I hope, will be only the beginning of a lifelong journey. Most of us start riding for practical reasons. A bicycle is cheap, and upkeep costs little; you don't have to pay tax or insurance, and you spend nothing on fuel. When you're unlucky with punctures and mechanical problems, repairs are economical, and even in a bad year, your outlay on parts and maintenance will be a fraction of what car, bus or train travel would cost you. There's also the speed and convenience. In rush-hour traffic, a bicycle will nearly always beat a taxi, car or bus, and it's door-to-door too: no more waiting for Tubes, trams or trains.

Those practical reasons are enough for many people, and that's fine. But there is much more to love about cycling. It is not only cheap, but cheerful too, making us happier as we ride. It gives our brain power a measurable boost, and makes our bodies stronger and fitter. Finally, there are the many environmental benefits – not only for the air we breathe, but also for the towns and cities we live in, and for the world's climate.

I hope this book will inspire you to cycle for pleasure, as well as out of necessity, so it ends with some ideas for taking you and your bike a little further from home. If this slim volume encourages anyone to ride more, ride further or ride for the first time, its author will be happy indeed.

PART ONE

Ready for the Road

Some of us have rediscovered a bike that has been left unridden in the shed for many years. Others have bought one second-hand, or scrounged one from a friend. It will become your trusted companion, but you must give it a check-up so it's ready for the road again.

This chapter covers the key components that most often need attention: chain, gears, brakes and wheels. It applies just as well to what you'll find on a folding bike as to traditional models.

Very often it takes just a few moments to transform your ride. Lubricate your chain, pump up your tyres, tune your gears and brakes, and you'll be amazed at how quickly and quietly you will zip about town. In this chapter we will also discuss how to clean your bike and how to make the most common quick fixes.

The anatomy of the bicycle

This chapter is *not* a complete repair or maintenance manual. Instead, it introduces the key components of the bike so that you can check them before you start riding and make minor adjustments as necessary. Below is the type of bike you're most likely to encounter; most parts labelled here are present on all bikes.

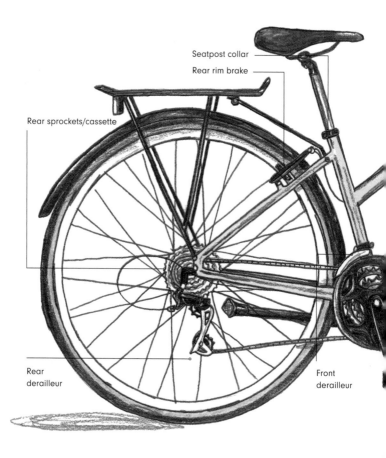

Seatpost collar

Rear rim brake

Rear sprockets/cassette

Rear derailleur

Front derailleur

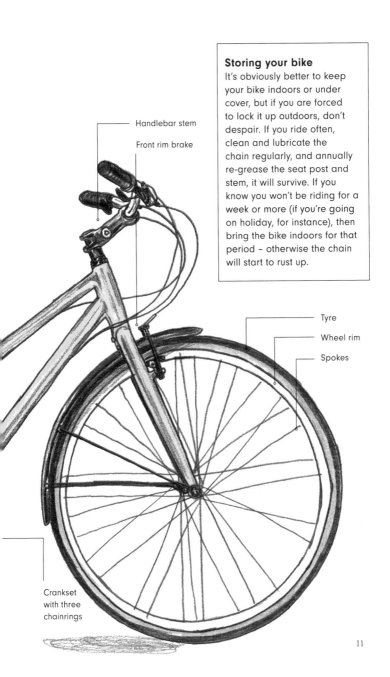

Handlebar stem

Front rim brake

Storing your bike
It's obviously better to keep your bike indoors or under cover, but if you are forced to lock it up outdoors, don't despair. If you ride often, clean and lubricate the chain regularly, and annually re-grease the seat post and stem, it will survive. If you know you won't be riding for a week or more (if you're going on holiday, for instance), then bring the bike indoors for that period – otherwise the chain will start to rust up.

Tyre

Wheel rim

Spokes

Crankset
with three
chainrings

11

Basic tools and lubricants

A full bike workshop has all manner of rarely used, heavy-duty tools, but for everyday maintenance you'll be able to get by with a fairly small selection.

Chain lubricant: A bottle of lube lasts a long time: you should apply it regularly, but only in small amounts. If your bike is often locked up outdoors, choose wet-weather lube, which will last longer.

Silicone grease: Grease will keep the hidden parts of your bike healthy. Put a dab on the thread of every bolt you tighten, and smear it on your seat post.

Track pump and small handheld pump: Get a track pump (also known as a floor pump) to keep at home – it will make your life so much easier – and have a small, handheld pump with you for emergencies. Make sure your pump has the right head for your tyres; there are two kinds, Presta and Schrader. (Many modern pumps, usefully, fit both.)

Multitool with a selection of hex keys: This will get you through most roadside repairs and simple jobs. Some have a spoke-adjusting tool too: so much the better. Hex keys are also known as Allen keys.

Screwdrivers: You need two – a flat-head and Phillips-head. Useful for tuning gears and fitting lights and bells.

Small adjustable wrench: For those bolts that don't have a hex head. Also known as a monkey wrench or plumber's wrench.

Spoke-adjusting tool: These usually have several apertures – make sure that one of them fits snugly around your spoke nipples.

Tyre levers: Get two – stout plastic, and hooked at one end.

Cleaning your bike

A clean bike goes faster – it's a fact. Well, maybe not, but it certainly feels that way. Cleaning your bike will definitely help it to last longer (it will corrode less), stop the parts from jamming up and make it look way better. It also encourages you to have a close look at everything, and can flag up any problems.

Always clean your bike outside. It's very tempting to get the hose out to blast all the gunk off, but don't do this! Under pressure, water will be forced into the joints and bearings, causing corrosion, and you really don't want that. Instead, use a bucket of warm soapy water and a sponge, and gently wipe and scrub everything until it's shining and bright again. Use an old toothbrush to get mud out of nooks and crannies. If your sprockets or derailleurs have particularly stubborn grease on them, use chain degreaser or a solution of citrus detergent to wash it off.

Don't worry about splashing soapy water on any parts of your bike; they will dry out and be fine. But don't leave your chain wet and unlubricated because it will rust, so give it a little extra care at the end of the job.

Cleaning and lubricating the chain

This is the easiest way to make your bike run dreamily smooth. You can do it using regular detergent (a solution of whatever you use to clean the floor: apply with an old rag, scrub the chain until it shines, then rinse off), but a specialist citrus-based chain cleaner is much quicker and easier to use, and you don't need to rinse it off. Use a rag and an old toothbrush to work it into dirty links. Always clean the chain's lower horizontal length, moving it along with the crank as you go so that the gunk you scrub off falls on to the ground, not on to a part you've just cleaned.

When the chain is clean, apply chain lube sparingly (a tiny drop on each link is enough) and give it a few backward spins of the cranks to disperse it around the links. Wipe any excess off the outer surface.

Checking the tyres

Tyres lose air over time, and inevitably wear out, so check them whenever you ride and top them up with a brief pump every few weeks.

Tyre pressure
Pinch each tyre firmly with your finger and thumb. You should be able to squash it, but only just, and not by much. When you're riding, your tyre should not splay outwards where it meets the road. Add air if it does. Most tyres have the maximum pressure marked on the side of the tyre.

Tyre condition
Look out for bald spots on the tread, and loose threads on the side of the tyre. If you see these, you'll need to replace the tyre as soon as possible.

16

Checking the rear derailleur

The rear derailleur moves the chain from the largest sprockets on the back wheel (low gear) to the smallest (high gear). On your first ride of any new bike, make sure that you can move quickly through all the available gears, and that changes are predictable. If the chain 'jumps' when you're not expecting it to, it needs replacing. If the chain falls off into the spokes, replace it on the sprocket, then adjust the low limit screw (marked 'L'); if it crunches into the chain stay, adjust the high limit screw (marked 'H'). If you can't engage your lowest gear, try turning the barrel adjuster once anticlockwise; if you can't engage your highest, turn it once clockwise.

Note that derailleurs don't move the chain when you're not pedalling – so before you halt, shift down into a low gear, ready for when you set off again.

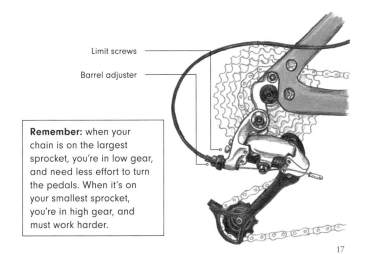

Limit screws

Barrel adjuster

Remember: when your chain is on the largest sprocket, you're in low gear, and need less effort to turn the pedals. When it's on your smallest sprocket, you're in high gear, and must work harder.

Checking the front derailleur

Not every bike has a front derailleur. This is a simple mechanism that rarely gives trouble, moving the chain from the small chainring on the crankset (low gear) to the large (high gear) while you pedal, and increasing the range of gears that you can choose from. Some cranksets have three chainrings, which is very useful on hills or off-road. To check yours, pedal with your rear derailleur set to a middle gear, then change up and down using the left-hand shifter on your handlebars.

In use, try not to 'cross-gear'. This is when you run the chain over the largest sprockets, front and back, simultaneously, or over the smallest sprockets, front and back, simultaneously. It strains the chain and causes horrible grinding or rubbing noises. To solve the problem, shift the rear derailleur towards a middle sprocket.

Hub gear maintenance

Hub gears, which usually give you a range of three gears but can go up to fourteen, are marvels of mechanical engineering. They are incredibly reliable, need no maintenance and, being protected by their shell, last forever. In order to work well, though, they need lubrication, and different models have different requirements. Find the make and model on the casing, check online what the manufacturer recommends, and make a note of what lubricant it needs, how to apply it, and how often.

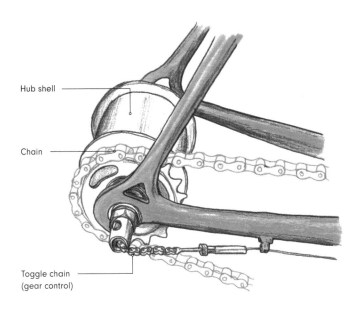

Hub shell

Chain

Toggle chain
(gear control)

Checking the brake levers

Cabled brakes work when you grip on the lever; this pulls on a cable, which, at the other end, forces brake pads on to the wheel. Check that the levers are well positioned and exert enough power. If you have small hands, you can bring the lever closer to the handlebars by tightening the adjustment screw. Pull hard on each lever; it should not touch the handlebar, or you won't be able to exert firm pressure on the brakes. If you need more braking power, tighten the cable by rotating the barrel adjuster (at the end of the cable housing) anticlockwise.

Some high-end bikes are fitted with hydraulic brakes, which are not covered in this book. Refer to the manufacturer's instructions if that's what you have.

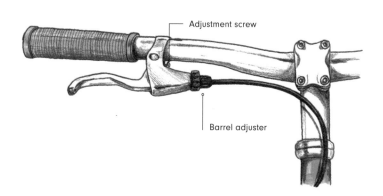

Adjustment screw

Barrel adjuster

Checking the brake pads

Most urban bikes have rim brakes that press brake pads on to the wheel when you pull on the levers. These pads are made of rubber or plastic and wear out in use, losing stopping power, so you must replace them in good time.

Check them by looking closely to see if the tread pattern has been worn flat. If so, replace them as soon as you can. Brake pads, and the shoes they sit in, come in different shapes and sizes; replace like with like at your local bike shop. Positioning new brake pads so that they press squarely on the rim, not the tyre, can take some time and fiddling, so be patient.

Safe brake pads

Dangerously worn brake pads

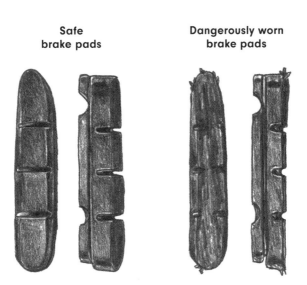

Caliper brakes

Caliper brakes grip the rim when the cable that connects them to the lever is pulled. The cable then retracts into the cable housing, pulling the two caliper arms together. To bring the pads closer to the rim (for instance, if they are slightly worn down), tighten the barrel adjuster (at the lever end, or at the caliper end of the cable) anticlockwise. To replace the pads, loosen the cable clamp, opening the calipers completely.

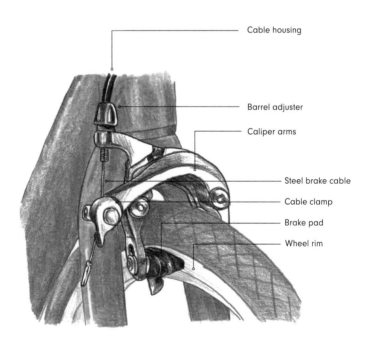

Cable housing

Barrel adjuster

Caliper arms

Steel brake cable

Cable clamp

Brake pad

Wheel rim

Cantilever (or V-) brakes

Often fitted to cheaper mountain bikes, cantilever brakes grip the rim when the cable that connects them to the lever is pulled. The cable then retracts into a metal 'noodle', pulling the two arms together. To bring the pads closer to the rim (for instance, if they are slightly worn down), tighten the barrel adjuster (at the lever end of the cable) one revolution anticlockwise. To replace brake pads, grip the levers closed and unclip the noodle from its housing, opening the levers completely.

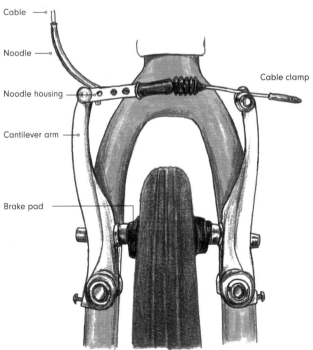

Cable

Noodle

Noodle housing

Cantilever arm

Brake pad

Cable clamp

Disc brakes

The most powerful brakes, these work by squeezing pads on to a metal disc when the cable that connects them to the lever is pulled. If you need more stopping power from them, rotate the barrel adjuster one revolution (or more if necessary) anticlockwise.

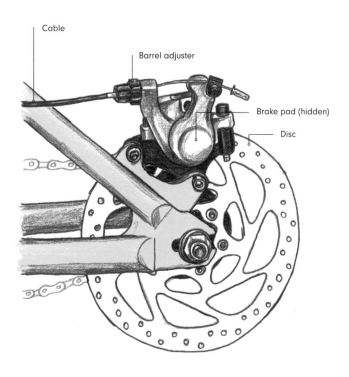

Cable

Barrel adjuster

Brake pad (hidden)

Disc

Checking the cranks

With the pedals mounted at their ends, the cranks rotate around a bearing called the bottom bracket (BB). There are many, many different kinds of crank and BB unit. Check that yours is healthy by pulling sideways on the crank arms. If there is any wobble, they must be tightened. Pay attention to this when you ride; wobbling cranks won't stop you getting about, but they will grind into your BB and, in time, destroy it.

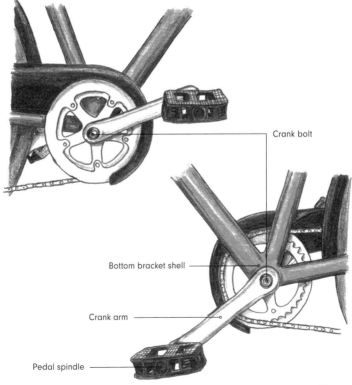

Crank bolt

Bottom bracket shell

Crank arm

Pedal spindle

25

Saddle and handlebar height

Many new cyclists have their saddle set too low or too high. There is one excellent reason to make sure it's at the right height: pain.

If the saddle is too low, your knees won't open properly when you're pedalling, and will become stiff. If your saddle is too high, your backside will move left and right across it, causing saddle sores. Fortunately, it's easy to find the right height.

First, you should remove and grease the seat post so it doesn't corrode and get stuck in the frame. With a hex (Allen) key or wrench, loosen the seat-tube bolt at the point where the post enters the frame, take out the seat post, and apply a light coating of grease along the length of the tube. A toothpaste-sized blob should be enough. Replace the seat post with the saddle pointing straight ahead, and tighten the seat-tube bolt.

Sit on the bike next to a wall so that you can support yourself, then pedal backwards until one crank is pointing straight down. When you place your heel on the centre of the pedal, your leg should be dead straight (see illustration opposite). To adjust the height, loosen the seat-tube bolt slightly, work the saddle up or down as necessary, tighten it and try again.

When you think the saddle is at the right height, double-check by placing the ball of your foot on the pedal, as you would when riding. When the crank is pointing straight down, your leg should be very slightly bent.

Once your saddle is set, experiment to find the best handlebar height. Most people find that bars at the same height as the saddle work well, but feel free to try them lower or higher. On many bikes, the bar height is adjusted by loosening the bolt in the middle of the stem using a hex key; sometimes you can adjust the angle of the stem itself too.

Lights, and where to put them

One of the best inventions of recent years is the rechargeable LED lamp that can either flash or shine continuously.

Bike lights used to be heavy and cumbersome, and frequently demanded expensive new batteries. Fortunately, these days you can charge up lighter, brighter, cheaper LED lamps and pop them into your bag; you'll hardly notice that they're there.

Entry-level lights usually fit using a rubber band that is easily stretched around the saddle post or handlebar; some can also be clipped on to your bag, pannier, jacket or helmet. In general, it's better to have the lights high up, which makes you more visible. In any case, always use them when cycling between dusk and dawn.

The home mechanic

I hope this chapter has demystified your bike, and given you the confidence to maintain it. At some point, though, something will go wrong. A crucial part will wear or break, or a mysterious squeaking noise will demand your attention, and you will have to get your hands dirty fixing your machine and getting it back on the road.

Learn to love this moment, and try to make the repair yourself before taking it to a shop. Below are three of the most common repairs you may have to attempt, but if something else goes wrong, you'll find that acquiring the new skills you need to fix your bike yourself is profoundly satisfying. There's nothing better than riding a smooth-running, near-silent bicycle and knowing that you made it so.

What you need

Invest in a basic repair manual, the necessary tools and lubricants, and get to know the excellent online resources that exist. A YouTube search for the problem will usually throw up a host of friendly instructional videos that you can follow to make the repair. I'm a fan of the ParkTool and Global Cycling Network channels, although there are many other knowledgeable mechanics also offering their expertise for free. Watch a couple of videos all the way through before you start work so that you know exactly how each repair or replacement should proceed.

Where to go when you get stuck

If you are lucky enough to have a community bike workshop nearby, use it! The people there won't fix your bike for you, but they will guide you through the process, letting you develop your own skills, and will have access to supplies of spare and second-hand parts too. Workshops like this are also a great introduction to the local cycling scene.

When you need to buy parts, use your local independent bike shop. Its prices may be slightly higher than online alternatives, but you'll certainly miss it if it's forced to close.

Changing an inner tube

At some point you will have to change your tyre's inner tube. As with any repair, the first time is tricky, but it gets easier and quicker with practice.

1

If you've just had a puncture, check the tread of the tyre to see if the offending object is still in place. If you find it, note where it went in, then pull it out.

2

Turn the bike upside down. Take the wheel off using the quick-release skewers or a wrench, then unscrew the cap and locknut from the inner tube's valve. Let any remaining air out of the tube.

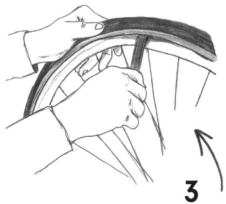

3

Work your fingers around the wheel, unsticking the bead (edge) of the tyre away from the rim on both sides.

Insert the point of a tyre lever inside the rim and under the tyre bead. Hook the other end around a spoke so that it stays in place.

4

Insert a second lever in the same way a handspan or two from the first one. The bead of the tyre should pop out of the rim between the two levers. If it doesn't do so immediately, try inserting the second lever closer to the first.

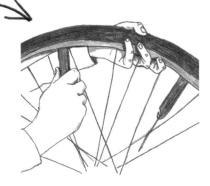

5

Grip the wheel firmly with one hand, unhook one of the levers and sweep it around the wheel so that its point scoops the tyre bead out of the rim. Work the valve out through its hole and remove the tube from the tyre.

6

If you have a spare inner tube, fit it now, and take the punctured one home to repair at your leisure. If you haven't, fix the puncture according to the instructions on pages 34–35.

7

Before you put a new tube in, run your fingers around the inside of the tyre and the rim to check that whatever it was that punctured your tyre is gone. Have another look at the outside if you don't find anything.

Take the new tube (or the same tube, once you've patched it) and insert the valve through its hole, making sure the inner tube at that point is enclosed by the tyre. Work the inner tube into the tyre all the way round.

8

Screw the locknut on to the valve, but don't tighten it down. Pump a little air into the tube so that it holds its shape but isn't stiff.

9

With your thumbs, and starting at the valve, start bedding the tyre back into the wheel rim. Do this with both hands at the same time, facing the wheel.

When you've done the first half, rotate the wheel and start working your hands towards each other until nearly all the tyre bead is bedded back into the rim.

10

A final stretch of about 15 cm may be tricky. If it is, take the tyre lever and reach the point under the tyre bead so that it engages with the wheel rim, then push it up so that the bead snaps in. Wetting the rim with a little water may lubricate it.

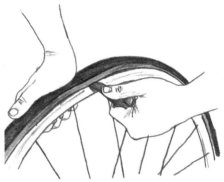

 Important: make sure you don't pinch the inner tube under the tyre!

Fixing a puncture

It's a good idea to fix punctures when you can, instead of buying a new inner tube each time.

The easiest to repair are those caused by a large object, such as a nail or a thorn; tiny slow punctures can be difficult to locate, and a puncture near the valve can be impossible to fix. In that case – or if your tube has been patched many times already – you should replace the tube.

1

Make yourself comfortable and have your pump and repair kit handy. First, find the hole or holes in the tube. You may find it necessary to pump the tube up a little to create the hiss that will help you.

2

When you've found a hole, mark it with the crayon in the repair kit. Then check around it in case there's another; if you had a 'pinch flat' from hitting a pothole, there will be two holes. Mark that one too.

3

Use the sandpaper in the kit to scuff the surface of the inner tube around the hole. Make sure the area you scuff is larger than the patch you will fit.

4

Apply a small blob of glue to the area, spread it around and wait for it to dry (follow the instructions on the tube). Again, make sure that the glued area is larger than the patch you will apply.

5

When the glue is dry, peel the foil from the patch, taking care not to touch the exposed sticky side. Apply the patch, pressing it firmly around the edges so that they stick down on the tube. Wait a couple of minutes for the patch to adhere, then carefully peel off the plastic film.

6

Rub a dusting of chalk over the whole repair so that the tube doesn't stick to the inside of your tyre, and insert the tube following the instructions on pages 32–33.

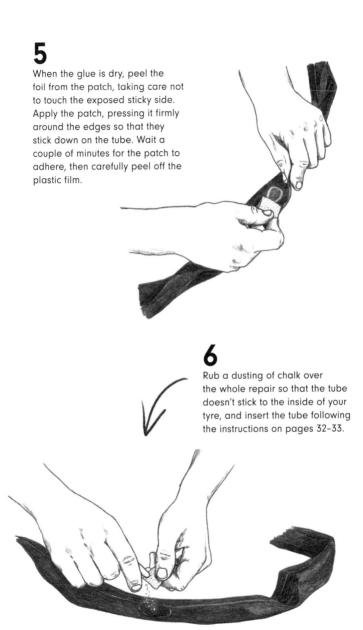

Straightening a bent wheel

The bicycle wheel is one of the most elegant of all inventions. A collection of flexible parts that are bound together into a rigid, strong whole, the wheel not only supports a huge load relative to its own weight, but also channels the entire force of your acceleration and braking. It's no surprise that sometimes a wheel bends in use, but it can usually be fixed.

Bicycle mechanics talk of making a wheel 'true', which is a beautiful way of saying 'straight'. It's not something you can improvise, and it needs focus, but if you don't rush, it's easy, and the most satisfying of repair jobs. Here's how to do it.

Noticing a bent wheel

Wheels in regular use sometimes go out of true slowly, but often it's after a bump – when you hit a pothole or kerb too fast. Whatever the cause, if you can feel (or hear) your wheel rim regularly touching your brake pads as you ride, you've got a kink. Time to straighten it out.

How wheels work: Spoke tension and nipples

Take a moment to understand your wheel. The spokes hook into the hub at the centre, and are screwed into the outer rim. At the point where a spoke meets the rim you will see a small bolt or 'nipple'. These sit in the rim, and the spokes, which are threaded, screw into them. By rotating the nipple you can, therefore, tighten or loosen each spoke. Spoke nipples come in different profiles, which is why spoke tools have differently shaped apertures. Experiment until you find the one that grips your spokes' nipples snugly.

1

Locate any loose spokes

Pluck all the spokes on the wheel (as you would a harp) to make sure they are evenly tensioned and give you a similar note. If one is loose, tighten its nipple with anticlockwise turns of the spoke tool until it feels about as tense as the other spokes (producing a similar tone when plucked).

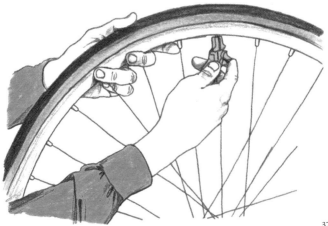

2

Locate and mark the kink

Turn the bike upside-down, resting on saddle and handlebars, and spin the wheel while looking along it. If you watch the rim where it passes between the brake calipers, you will see the kink projecting once every rotation. Take a pencil and, while the wheel spins, gradually move the point towards the rim so that the tip brushes the top of the kink, marking the area you need to adjust.

From the marked side of the wheel, observe whether the mark on the rim is closest to a spoke that terminates on the same side of the hub, or on the far side. If the same side, refer to Step 3a below; if the far side, see Step 3b.

3A

Spoke terminates on the same side

Loosen the spoke nearest the mark by turning the nipple half a revolution clockwise.

Now tighten the two neighbouring spokes by turning each nipple a quarter of a revolution anticlockwise. Spin the wheel to check whether the kink has gone. If not, repeat this step until it has.

Hub

Far side spoke

Near side spoke

Pencil mark

Far side spoke

3B

Spoke terminates on the far side

Loosen the two spokes to either side of the mark by turning each nipple half a revolution clockwise.

Now tighten the spoke nearest to the mark by turning the nipple a quarter of a revolution anticlockwise.

Spin the wheel to check whether the kink has gone. If not, repeat this step until it has.

Hub

Near side spoke

Far side spoke

Pencil mark

Near side spoke

These diagrams show simplified spoke arrangements – on your bike they probably cross over each other. You don't need to worry about this; just note which side of the wheel hub the spoke is attached to.

> **⚠ If in doubt, stop!**
> It is easy to make a kink worse by over-adjusting the spoke tension. Keep track of the adjustments you make, and don't be afraid to reverse them and retrace your steps.

PART TWO

Riding Safely, Riding Confidently

Let's be honest: bike riding in cities and towns can be scary. The good news is that if you learn how to look after yourself on a bike, it will quickly feel a lot safer.

Now your bike's ready to roll, you need to get yourself ready too. In this chapter, we'll look at preparation, equipment and clothing before looking at riding in traffic, with illustrations showing you the safest way to ride, and the latest research on traffic safety and driver behaviour.

A confident attitude is key. After all, you have as much right to the road as anyone else does.

Learning to ride
for the first time

Proverbially, we never forget how to ride a bike; even after years out of the saddle, it's a skill that comes back very quickly. But what if you never learned to ride as a child? How do you master it as an adult? Happily, the answer is simple – but also a little counter-intuitive.

The skill of riding a bike is a trick of balance, and it's not the kind of ability that you can pick up from a YouTube tutorial. A bike is balanced by a series of tiny left–right steers, and these moves are made on a subconscious level, with the rider hardly aware that they are making them. Although it's not very helpful to say 'the only way to learn how to ride a bike is to ride a bike', really the only way to master this balancing is to sit on a moving bike and do it. Happily, there is an elegant solution that lets you master the art of balance without fear. It's simple: all you have to do is take the pedals off.

    If you sit on a bike without pedals and with both feet on the ground, you can push it forwards easily with your feet and start cruising along, initially at walking pace but then faster and faster.

Getting going

The best place to do this is a level, paved surface with no traffic. A quiet car park is ideal, the larger the better. Remove the pedals from the cranks using a wrench (or a hex key if there is a recess for one on the spindle).

Make sure you can sit on the saddle with both feet on the ground at the same time; you should drop it to a lower level than you will later have it when riding. Put on your helmet, then just start to push yourself around, gaining speed until you can lift your feet from the ground.

You'll instinctively learn the small steers that keep you upright, and you'll discover that the faster you move, the steadier you feel. If you do lose your balance, all you have to do is put a foot down on the ground, and you won't fall. While doing all this, you can practise leaning into a turn, freewheeling and braking.

You'll be wobbly when you start, but persevere for a while, and when you are comfortable skimming around at jogging pace, steering in circles and braking to a controlled halt, you can reintroduce the pedals. Put them back on the bike, then make sure that you are in first gear. Set the crank of your stronger foot so that it's pointing up and forwards, and push off.

> **⚠ Important:**
> The pedal on the left-hand side has a reverse thread. It unscrews with clockwise turns, and tightens anticlockwise.

Essential skills

Once you're moving, don't stop! Keep pedalling and keep moving, steering and braking and freewheeling. As you feel more confident, practise shifting up and down through the gears, making sure you are always in low gear when you come to a halt. You'll soon find that you are in complete control. Adjust the saddle so that it's at the right height for riding, not cruising (see pages 26–27), then ride for a while until you're used to this new position. In particular, carry on until you are able to quickly look left and right, and back over your shoulder, without wobbling the bike, because this is an essential survival skill on the road. You must be able to make hand signals too, so practise riding one-handed with the other arm fully extended for a few seconds at a time.

When you're happy that you can start, stop, steer, change gear, look around and make hand signals without losing control, you can build up your skill and confidence on quiet roads that you already know well.

Feet and pedals

Pay attention to where your feet are on the pedals. The ball of each foot should be right in the middle, above the spindle. This is the most efficient and comfortable position, but it takes a little getting used to.

Teaching a child to ride

You can use the same 'pedal-free' method with children. Don't be distracted by the 'stabilizers' or training wheels that are often supplied with kids' bikes; they won't help. Completely ineffective, they actually stop the child from learning how to balance, and also restrict the range of manoeuvres the bike can make because they prevent the rider from leaning into a turn – thereby rendering the bike inherently unstable, and causing unnecessary falls. Just take the pedals off, and everything becomes a lot easier. Make sure, before the child starts cruising around, that the saddle height allows them to rest both feet on the ground at once.

Racks, bags, baskets and panniers

You'll need to carry stuff when you ride, and it's much better to load up the bike than yourself.

It is, of course, possible to ride with a backpack or shoulder bag, but it's far from ideal. Riding tends to warm you up, so a rucksack will make your back uncomfortably hot and sweaty, and you need to be able to turn your body to look around, which makes a heavy shoulder bag swing alarmingly. So if you carry anything bigger than a handbag, you should load it on your bike.

Luggage rack

A rack, or carrier, over the rear wheel can carry a surprising amount: it's essential. Get a couple of hooked elastic bungee cords and you'll find that quite large bags, boxes and parcels can be carried safely if you lash them down tightly. You can get racks that sit over the front wheel too.

Panniers

These are must-have partners for your rack. Get a pair of large waterproof rear panniers and you'll find that you can get a supermarket shop home without trouble. Front panniers on the forks are more useful for touring than everyday riding.

Rack bag

Sitting on top of the rear carrier, many rack bags expand to reveal pannier bags that can be folded out to increase their capacity.

Basket or bar bag

This is the handiest way to carry small loads, and has the advantage of being right where you can access it.

Saddle bags, frame bags, stem bags ...

There is a huge variety of ingenious smaller bags that can increase your capacity if you're touring.

Child seats, trailers and tow-alongs

Sharing the ride with the people (or pets) you love the most gives your ride an extra dimension. There are three excellent ways of bringing your children along: in a seat on your bike, behind you in a trailer, or on a tow-along. Whichever way you choose, you'll find that motorists tend to give more consideration to a bike with passengers than to a bike without.

Child seats
Mounted over the rear wheel, a seat can carry a child up to the age of 4 or 5. It will have straps and a robust shell to protect the occupant, and you'll find that you can strike up conversations with them on the way to nursery. Hills can be hard work, though.

Trailers

Pulled behind the bike, a trailer can carry one or two children – or dogs, or a good deal of shopping. A bike with a trailer requires less effort than one with a seat, and also shelters the passenger(s) from the elements. Fit a pennant and extra lights to be seen and safe.

Tow-alongs

Once a child is big enough to sit safely on a saddle, a tow-along bike trains them how to cycle safely – and their pedalling can help you along too! As with trailers, a pennant and extra lights will make sure you are both visible.

Fitting your helmet

If you're riding on the road, you should wear a helmet. No one likes to, but if you're knocked off your bike, it may save your life. It's pointless to wear a helmet that doesn't protect your head, so make sure it's properly fitted.

Adjust the straps so that they don't cover your ears, and so that the clip is under your chin (not against the end of it). You should be able to fit your index finger into the gap between strap and neck. The padding should be snug around your skull, so tighten the helmet using the dial on the back until it is – you can do this while you're wearing it. The helmet should be horizontal and sit about two finger-widths above your eyebrows.

It should go without saying that a tilted-back helmet that leaves your forehead exposed won't help much if you do have an accident.

Perfect!

Not so good...

What to wear

There's nothing worse than getting soaked in a rainstorm on the morning commute, then having to dry off and warm up while you're trying to work. Just a few cheap additions to your wardrobe will make all the difference.

Cycling jackets have many features that make them much more comfortable than an everyday model. A dropped hem at the rear protects your bottom, pockets on the back are easy to reach when you're riding, and elasticated cuffs and collars keep wind and rain out. These jackets are also cut to be comfortable when you lean forwards, and most have reflective details that keep you safe in the dark. Get a breathable waterproof one to use year-round, and in cold weather, wear a thick jumper underneath.

It's easy to mock Lycra shorts and leggings, but they are by far the most comfortable legwear, giving your muscles and joints freedom of movement and cool air. In wet weather, they dry off more quickly than trousers, and the padded seat makes your saddle much more comfortable.

Sunglasses will also keep wind and rain out of your eyes, and zipped waterproof overshoes are essential for wet winter rides, keeping your feet blissfully warm and dry. Padded gloves smooth out the 'buzz' from a rough road surface.

Finally, remember that there's no such thing as bad weather – only the wrong clothes.

Choosing a lock

It's a sad truth that bikes are vulnerable to theft, especially in big cities, so investing in a decent lock to deter thieves is essential.

If you want to be able to leave your bike for a few hours without worrying, you need as a minimum a D-lock made of solid steel. Choose something from a respected brand, such as ABUS or Kryptonite, keep its mechanism oiled, and don't skimp; a lock that deters thieves effectively will save you a lot of trouble – and money – in the long run.

Keep a safe note of the key number so that you can order replacements if you lose the keys it comes with. An additional cable with looped ends will allow you to secure both wheels at once, for extra security; this is useful if you have to lock up your bike overnight in a public space (see page 78).

Heavy-duty steel chains and padlocks can also be secure, but they are much heavier and more cumbersome to carry around. If you regularly secure your bike in the same spot, you can leave a lock there full time to save the effort of carrying it about. Avoid cheap combination locks on steel cables, as these offer little protection.

Before every ride

It takes just a couple of seconds to check that your bike is ready to go, and it's an easy habit to get into. The two essential checks to make, every time you ride, are your tyres and your brakes.

Check the tyres

Before you get on, give each tyre a firm pinch. If they feel squashy, or if you can compress them by more than 5 mm or so, it's time to get the pump out. You'll be able to ride on soft tyres, but they will wear out more quickly, it's tiring, and it leaves you much more vulnerable to flats.

Check the brakes

You *really* don't want your brakes to fail in traffic. Stand over the crossbar, pull hard on the front brake lever and push firmly forwards on the handlebars. You should not be able to roll the front wheel at all, and the bike shouldn't budge. Repeat with the rear brake; the bike may move slightly, but the rear wheel shouldn't rotate.

If either wheel rotates, check the brake pads, and if they're worn out, replace them as soon as you can. If the pads are OK, just tighten the barrel adjusters with a half-turn anticlockwise. Check again and repeat if necessary.

Loading up

If you are carrying luggage, try to load it symmetrically to keep your bike balanced. Two half-full panniers are much easier to ride with than a single full one.

Lights: to flash or not to flash?

Make sure you have a charged front and back lamp with you if you plan to be out after sundown. Research shows that flashing rear lights make motorists notice you from further away, but a continuous beam makes it easier for them to judge your position accurately. Ideally, therefore, you should sport two rear lamps, one set to flash, the other shining continuously.

Puncture repair kit

This is so light and cheap that you can afford to keep one in the bottom of your pannier just in case. Don't forget that you will also need tyre levers and, if your wheels don't have quick-release skewers, the right wrench to remove them.

Know your rights

You'll be a much more confident cyclist if you know your rights and aren't afraid to exercise them, but the sad truth is that very few drivers – or cyclists – actually know the law as it pertains to cycling.

Rights and responsibilities

Many motorists are of the mistaken belief that driving a car or van gives them some kind of priority on the road. It doesn't. We all have rights as road users, and – apart from bike-free motorways and similar A roads – we have to share the space respectfully, carefully and lawfully. All road users should respect the Highway Code, which overlaps with UK law.

Overtaking

The Highway Code states that a motorist should overtake a cyclist exactly as they would another car: that is, they should move over to the other side of the road to do so (Rule 163). That means that any motorist who whizzes past without giving you plenty of space is in breach of the law. They should also (Rule 162) overtake only if there is clear road ahead, and not cut in when they return to their side of the road (Rule 163 again). Overtaking a cyclist and immediately making a left turn across their path, which unfortunately is common, is therefore forbidden too.

Primary position

First, feel confident that you can ride down the middle of the lane, in what is called primary position, the same line taken by motor vehicles. British Cycling advises:

> Contrary to what inexperienced cyclists may think, this is where they are often safer, as it is where they can most easily see and be seen. Trainees should be encouraged to think like a driver of a vehicle, and if in doubt position themselves where a vehicle would be. Riding in the primary position is sometimes called 'taking the lane', as the cyclist takes the position normally taken by the motorist, who is thus prevented from attempting to overtake.

However, there are times when you should, out of consideration for your fellow road users, move over towards the kerb:

> When riding in the primary position, trainees should travel at a reasonable speed, as part of the traffic flow. If, however, traffic is building up behind them and the road ahead is clear, they may wish to move to the secondary position to avoid obstructing other road users unnecessarily.

Cycle lanes

If there is a cycle lane next to the road, you can use it, but you don't have to if you don't want to. Nor do you have to wear a helmet (but see page 96 for why you should).

Riding two abreast

This is completely legal (Rule 66), but riding three abreast isn't. On a narrow or busy road, cyclists should ride in single file. If the fact that you are riding two abreast on a normal road means that a motorist has to wait to overtake, they shouldn't be overtaking anyway (Rule 163 again).

Careful driving

Three further rules in the Highway Code (211, 212, 213) specify that drivers should 'be especially careful' around cyclists, 'give them plenty of room' and pay particular attention in case they 'suddenly need to avoid uneven road surfaces and obstacles such as drain covers or oily, wet or icy patches on the road'. Most drivers heed this. Not all do.

Road tax

When expressing their frustration at being trapped in an unhealthy metal box, motorists occasionally tell you that because they 'pay road tax' they enjoy some kind of priority on the road. They do not pay road tax. No one does; it has not existed since 1937! Motorists do, however, pay Vehicle Excise Duty – a car tax – which is a levy on the emissions and pollution their cars create.

Honour your responsibilities

Respect red lights
A common grumble of resentful motorists is that cyclists 'always jump red lights', breaking Rule 71 in the Highway Code. It is undeniably true that you frequently see cyclists doing so, endangering themselves and other people in the act. Don't be that person.

Pavements
Another common sight is cyclists riding along pedestrian pavements. Usually it is teenage boys or young men who do this; I've never worked out if they're motivated more by a fear of traffic, or an obnoxious desire to assert themselves, but I suspect it's the latter. Don't do it yourself, obviously. For a child up to the age of ten, riding on the pavement is not an offence.

Two brakes
For excellent reasons (rain; hills; pedestrians; mechanical failure), the law specifies that every bike must have two working sets of brakes. Some fashionable fixies (fixed-gear bikes with no freewheel capability) make do with one, but this is a rebellious style statement without practical merit. If your bike has only one set, fit another as a priority.

Indicating

Look behind before you indicate with your arms.
Do so conspicuously, and whenever you're about to
turn or manoeuvre.

Keeping cars distant

It's no fun when traffic whooshes past you at high speed
and only centimetres away. Fortunately, it's possible to ride
your bike – safely and legally – so that motorists give you
more space.

Researchers at Cycle Training UK discovered that
motorists tend to pass cyclists so that there is an equal
distance between them and the cyclist as there is between
the cyclist and the side of the road. Surprisingly, this gives
you some control over the situation: if you cycle 1–1.5
metres from the kerb – well out of the gutter – most
motorists will, subconsciously, give you about the same
clearance – a safe distance. Conversely, if you ride down
the gutter, they will give you less.

Passing motorists generally
give cyclists the same clearance
as the cyclist's own distance
from the kerb.

This real-world research runs counter to the advice of UK traffic police, who advise cyclists that drivers will give them 1.5 metres clearance if they cycle 0.75 metres out from the kerb. Unfortunately, drivers don't behave that way.

Staying out of the gutter has other advantages. You'll have fewer punctures, find more room to manoeuvre, be further away from unpredictable pedestrians, and throw up less gunk on to your shoes. Never go there if you can help it.

Studies have also shown that drivers tend to give more space to cyclists who don't wear helmets, who have long (stereotypically feminine) hair, or who have child seats on the back of their bikes.[1] There is no logic to this, of course, but that's how it is.

Finally, if you happen to be a motorist as well as a cyclist, then set an example for other drivers by bearing the rules in mind as you drive.

You exist!

There are times when you have to let people know that you're on the road too. This might be to avert a collision, or it might be to point out to someone that they are driving dangerously.

It's a curious phenomenon that new cyclists often care much more about their bell than other, much more critical, parts of their bike. Experienced riders rarely bother to fit a bell (now not a legal requirement in the UK), knowing that a well-timed shout tends to be more effective at getting the attention of the pedestrian who's about to walk out in front of you. It's true that a bell sounds friendly and non-aggressive, but then again, there's nothing to stop you from shouting in a good-natured way. Greet every straying jaywalker as if they are an old friend, with a cheery 'hiya', and you'll not only alert them to your presence, but maybe raise a smile.

When you get cut up

Undoubtedly the worst thing about cycling is being treated disrespectfully or dangerously by your fellow road users. This varies from close high-speed passes to reckless overtaking or sudden turns across your path, and near misses can be terrifying. When something like this happens, try to stay calm. The vast majority of these events are caused by carelessness, not malice; it may feel as though that driver was trying to kill you, but they probably weren't.

If you get the chance to speak to the driver about it, my view is that you should raise it with them if you can. That way, they may be more considerate of the next cyclist they come across. If you do manage to get their attention at the next traffic lights, start off by smiling, then politely ask them if they noticed you before they put your life at risk. Most will apologize at this point. Some will argue that cycle lanes are 'shared spaces', that 'motor vehicles have priority' or that 'I pay road tax, so it's my road.' All these points are wrong, and don't be afraid to say so, but do so politely. A few will skip apology or argument and escalate straight to verbal abuse. Don't rise to it; instead, conspicuously take a picture of their number plate, then cycle carefully away, leaving them to worry if you are going to report them.

The worst cases of dangerous driving should, of course, always be reported to the police. There are regularly convictions of drivers whose reckless or abusive behaviour has been captured by the helmet cams that some cyclists wear.

Braking

Your two brakes aren't equal in power, and you should practise until you're comfortable with the difference.

The front brake (right-hand lever)

This has all the power, so use it whenever you need to stop. When braking hard, brace your arms and move your weight back as far as possible. Practise rapid halts on a quiet road until you have learned to modulate the force you apply with the lever.

The rear brake (left-hand lever)

This has much less power, so use it to slow down gently, when approaching traffic lights, or controlling downhill speed. Avoid skids, which are fun but wear your tyres out.

Remember

A car can stop faster than you can. In moving traffic, leave plenty of space to brake into if a driver decides to stop unexpectedly.

Wet weather

Rain and standing water dramatically affect braking. If your rim brakes get wet, your stopping distance is tripled or more. To avoid terror, and collisions, ride more carefully. 'Feather' the brakes by frequently pressing them lightly so the pads sweep water off the rims; and if you are riding downhill, apply the brakes continuously to avoid picking up speed.

The right gear

You don't have to watch inexperienced cyclists for long to realize that gears are tricky and take a little practice.

Traffic lights can pose a difficulty; novice riders often stop at red in a high gear, then find that they are stuck in it when the lights change to green. This means a slow, wobbling start as the rider musters the necessary torque, or a horrible crunch of gears as they try to change down under load.

Practise changing down before reaching the lights – or anything else that will arrest your progress, be it a junction, stop sign or traffic jam. Move down through the gears from about 20 metres out so that you're in first when you stop. That will make it easy to start up again in a controlled way – quickly or slowly.

If you see that the lights ahead of you are red, slow down. Try to time it so that you coast up to them as they turn green, and then you won't have to stop at all.

If you have front and rear derailleurs and your gears are scraping or feel stiff, you may be cross-geared (see page 18). Remember not to ride with the chain on both of your largest sprockets (front and back) or both of the smallest sprockets.

Car doors

We are rightly careful about cars that are moving, and moving fast, but a parked vehicle can be the worst of all if its occupant decides to open the door without looking back to see who's coming. You have to keep your eyes open, just in case they don't.

When riding, pass parked cars by at least 1 metre (many car doors extend further than that, but this gives you crucial extra time and space to manoeuvre). Watch for exhaust smoke, movements inside parked vehicles, people getting out of a car kerbside, and faces in wing mirrors, which may give you an early warning.

Pedestrians

Although pedestrians are slow-moving and mostly predictable, they do occasionally make surprising moves.

Watch out for them on shopping streets, outside busy buildings and near bus stops, and be especially careful of people using mobiles or wearing headphones; they may be completely unaware that you are there. Be ready to slow down, take evasive action or stop.

Nearside turns in heavy traffic

This should be one of the easiest manoeuvres for cyclists and drivers alike, but in heavy traffic it can be dangerous.

The risk occurs when heavy vehicles, with poor visibility of cyclists riding kerbside, turn across their paths; they can easily knock a rider off, or squash them into street furniture.

As you approach a busy nearside turn, stay aware of what other vehicles' intentions are, assume that they cannot see you, and *do not overtake them on the inside.* Repeat: *do not overtake heavy vehicles on the inside.* Just wait the couple of seconds it takes for them to make their move. It may save your life.

NEVER, EVER undertake heavy vehicles on the inside as they may not be able to see you.

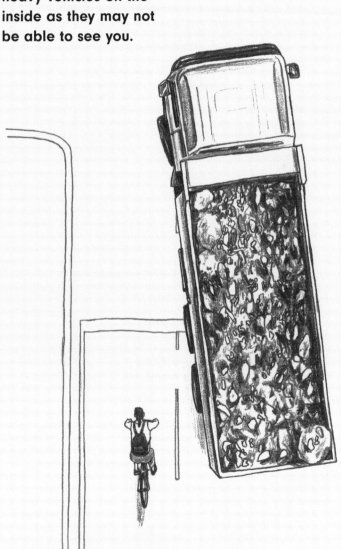

Working through traffic

Any city commuter on a bike will at some point have to pass between two lanes of stationary traffic. This is completely legal, and often the most sensible course to take: there is usually more space between two rows of cars than there is kerbside, where you will be forced into the gutter. When you're doing this, take particular care.

Pulling out

Before pulling out into the middle of the traffic jam, look twice, both ways, along the gap between the stuck lanes. Motorbikes, mopeds and other cyclists will all be using this space too.

Don't rush

Motorists in a traffic jam are in a stressful situation and may make surprising choices. Give yourself time to react by not going too fast, making yourself conspicuous, and not making sudden or unpredictable moves yourself.

Hang back

Buses frequently need to change lanes. Respect them, stop and let them do so; don't surprise the driver by squeezing through tiny gaps opened up by their manoeuvre.

Likewise, be wary around trucks, and overtake them only when you can be absolutely sure that you are visible in their mirrors. If you can't see the driver's face, they can't see you. If in any doubt, stop and wait for everyone to move on together.

Turning across traffic

Turning across traffic, particularly on a busy road when you are heavily laden, demands care.

As you approach your turn, look around so you know what's behind you, then signal and move out into the middle of the road when there's an opening. Be confident, signal conspicuously and make your intentions completely clear.

If there's no gap in the oncoming traffic and you have to wait in the middle of the road, make sure you are in low gear so that you can move off easily and without wobbling when there is a space.

Headphones

Music is wonderful, one of life's great pleasures. Listening to it playing loudly on headphones while cycling through traffic, however, is one of the most foolish things you can do.

Not only does it stop you from hearing what's coming up behind, which is crucial information if you enjoy staying on your bike (and alive), it also – if the music is any good – stops you from concentrating on the road ahead and what's coming up to meet you.

Another reason to unplug is that you will get more from your ride when fully engaged with the experience, not concentrating on the music in your head. As we will find later in this book, many of the mental benefits of cycling flow from the experience of being focused on the ride and lost in the moment.

That said, if your headphones don't block out external sounds, spoken-word radio and podcasts won't tune you out from your environment, and will compromise your safety much less than music.

If you really can't live without sound, you could do what an old friend of mine used to do on his commute across London. He worked in politics, and had to be across the morning news, so he rode in every day with a transistor radio playing in the basket on his handlebars.

Locking up

**Before you lock up, look around.
Is this spot busy? Is it well lit?**

Passing pedestrians, open shops, cafés, bus stops and street lights all deter thieves. If there are already plenty of locked bikes in the area, so much the better. Find a solid piece of metalware – a bike rack, railings or a street sign – that is concreted into the ground, and lock your bike to it.

If you have a D-lock, make sure it passes through both the frame and the front wheel at the same time (front wheels are stolen more often, despite the fact that a rear wheel is nearly as easy to remove and has greater value; bike thieves aren't that bright). Double-check before walking away, and don't forget to remove your lights. I usually leave my helmet clipped to the bike rather than carry it about, as people don't seem to value helmets enough to steal them.

For more security, or if you're leaving your bike out overnight, you will want more reassurance than a D-lock on its own. Use a stout cable with looped ends, and pass it through the rear wheel, frame and, if possible, the bike rack, looping the ends on to the D-lock.

PART THREE

Happy, Fit, Smart and Riding Towards a Better World

What exactly is it that makes cyclists happier? Why are they healthier than the rest of us? Why do they sleep better? And why are they more efficient and productive at work?

You will get much more out of riding your bike if you know why you enjoy it so much, if you understand the benefits for your body and mind, and if you can see the positive change that you make to your environment every time you ride.

This knowledge will transform your experience, turning cycling from a cheap, convenient mode of transport to a thought-provoking, mindfulness-inducing mental boost.

The happy cyclist

The next time you see a cyclist just as they arrive at their destination, be it home, the office or a café, take a good look at them. Their eyes will be bright, their cheeks will be flushed, and their body language will show that they're ready for anything: they'll be poised, alert, vigorous, awake – in a word, *alive*.

Even a ten-minute spin gives the rider this magical lift, and anyone who rides a bike will recognize it. But where does it come from?

The hormones of health and happiness

When we think of hormones, the negatives often come to mind first: we blame them for anger, tension, stress and other undesirable emotions. This isn't totally fair, however. Hormones also have strikingly positive effects, which regular cycling is known to amplify.

Anandamide

Also found in chocolate, this hormone boosts mood and is the source of the 'cyclist's high' experienced on a long ride, since it kicks in after about 30 minutes of moderate-intensity exercise. As well as short-term euphoria, it boosts happiness in the longer term.

Cortisol

This is part of the body's response to stress and its fight-or-flight reflex. Too much cortisol in the long term is very unhealthy, but the small amounts released by regular gentle exercise of up to an hour are good for you: anti-inflammatory, easing irritation and pain, and promoting good sleep.

Dopamine

This gives us a sense of satisfaction when we complete a task or exercise. It boosts focus, motivation, attention span and the ability to experience pleasure.

Norepinephrine

This plays a role in the sleep cycle, helping you to wake up, but it also increases focus, attention and the effectiveness of memory, and encourages the body to burn fat.

Serotonin

Stimulated by exercise and sunlight, serotonin makes us happy, reduces depression and helps us to sleep well. Taken together, the cocktail of hormones mixed by our bodies when we cycle is a potent brew for body and mind. In particular, the hormones benefit our sleep, especially if we ride during the first half of the day, and in sunlight. We also know that good sleeping patterns in turn make us fitter, so regular riding creates a virtuous circle of good rest and a healthy body.

Exercise and PMS
Complicated mechanisms, involving many hormones mentioned on these pages, affect the severity of premenstrual syndrome (PMS). A study by academics at Azad University, Isfahan, in 2013 found that eight weeks of regular exercise had a dramatic effect on symptoms experienced by women aged 18–25, reducing PMS by 60 per cent, physical symptoms by 65 per cent, and psychological symptoms by 52 per cent.[2] Three hours of cycling a week would be enough to have a similar effect.

Cycling as a hobby

Most of us come into cycling with purely practical intentions: we cycle to work, to the shops or to school, and when there is no reason to ride, we don't. There's nothing wrong with that, but cycling really comes into its own when we do it for fun.

Apart from maximizing the benefits of cycling that commuters already enjoy, riding for fun will open up new parts of your neighbourhood, whether you live in a huge city or in the deepest countryside. Riding with a friend, or joining a cycling club, gives this another dimension.

Learning the basics of cycle mechanics and then carrying out your own repairs and services is another route to happiness. Psychologists know that a constructive hobby of this type is a great way to find the 'flow' state of mind, that elusive, absorbing feeling of being happily lost in what you're doing, and not noticing the passing of time.

This valuable state is much, much better for your mental health than passive 'relaxation', so seek it out. The next time you're contemplating yet another evening of Netflix on the couch, why not tune your brakes and gears, or re-grease your bearings instead? You'll feel a lot better for it.

The mindful cyclist

Since mindfulness went mainstream, its benefits have become well known, and every day millions of us deliberately seek a mindful state through meditation or yoga. Some of us have spotted, too, that cycling, even through heavy traffic, is an inherently mindful activity. In order to stay upright, you have to remain constantly aware of your surroundings, and exist in the moment; if you don't, you'll fall off. Moreover, in the open air you are completely tuned into your environment and the natural world around you.

Richard Ballantine, one of the great opinionators on the subject of bikes, summarized this state of mind brilliantly in *Richard's Bicycle Book* (1972):

> *Now look at what happens to you on a bicycle. It's immediate and direct. You pedal. You make decisions. You experience the tang of the air and the surge of power as you bite into the road. You're vitalized. As you hum along, you fully and gloriously experience the day, the sunshine, the clouds, the breezes. You're alive!*

That's not to say, of course, that cycling is meditation, but it is definitely possible to benefit from cycling in some of the same ways. To turn your ride into a truly mindful experience, try some of the following ideas.

Be aware
Focus on your environment, paying attention to the noises surrounding you, from bird calls to car engines and the wind in your ears. With your gaze resting on the road ahead, watch the road surface, and register every bump and change in texture.

Observe your technique

Notice each rotation of your cranks, feel the force of your muscles as you push down through the balls of your feet, and make your pedal strokes even and smooth. Pedal in time with your breaths and reach an even, balanced cadence.

Notice your breath

Focus on your breathing, the movements of your diaphragm and the rush of air in and out of your body. Regulate your breathing so that each inhalation pulls you forwards to your destination, and each exhalation pushes down into your legs.

Think about your body

Pay attention to how each part of your body feels, from your feet to the top of your head. Don't judge: if your legs ache, notice the feeling, but don't assign it negative (or positive) qualities. Observe the temperature of your body, your heart rate, and which muscles are tense, which relaxed.

Ride yourself fitter

When you get a bike, you're effectively getting free gym membership. We all know that cycling is good cardiovascular exercise – as is any activity that raises the pulse – but you may be surprised by some of the other health benefits, from pain relief to a better immune system and a longer life. Believe it: cycling is *really* good for you. Here's why...

The muscles that do the work

The rotation that drives your bike forward draws on five muscle groups working in sequence. Starting with your pedal at the top of the stroke, and thinking of the crank as the hour hand of a clock, it goes:

1
Gluteus maximus
The largest muscle in the body, this starts the stroke off at the top of the dial, 12 o'clock. Working this muscle out regularly will give you well-toned buttocks.

2
Quadriceps
A group of four muscles across the front of each thigh. Picking up the stroke as your crank passes the 2 o'clock angle, these muscles provide most of your riding power.

3

Hamstring

Running up the back of each thigh, the hamstrings pull the pedal back up to 12 o'clock.

To make the best use of your muscles – especially if you ride for more than half an hour or so – you must make sure that your position is high enough and far enough forward for them to extend. Many beginners assume a position that is too low, and suffer stiffness and joint pain as a result.

4

Gastrocnemius and soleus

These muscles in your calves take the pedal down to its lowest point, taking the strain between 5 and 6 o'clock.

Core strength

While the leg muscles do the bulk of the work, our upper bodies play their part too. The constant tiny adjustments that keep us balanced improve posture and coordination, and develop our core fitness.

The core – the collection of muscles around our abdomen, back and waistline – keeps the body stable on the saddle. With a strong core, you cycle more efficiently; it stops your body rocking from side to side, so all the power produced by your legs goes down into the pedals. Apart from wasting energy, that rocking will also give you saddle sores, where your posterior rubs back and forth over the saddle. The core muscle groups also get pressed into use when you are hill-climbing, or standing on the pedals to generate a burst of power.

Serious racing cyclists, therefore, build up their core muscles in the gym. You'll probably find that your core will naturally gain strength as you ride every day, particularly if you focus on your posture and the smooth rotation of the pedals when the gluteus maximus and quadriceps kick in.

Better joints

Regular cycling will give your legs and buttocks excellent muscle tone, but it will also have benefits for the joints and soft tissues that hold muscle and skeleton together.

Cycling is a low-impact exercise that moves the joints, reducing stiffness, and increases blood flow around them, reducing pain and the symptoms of arthritis and rheumatism. Unlike running, or sports such as tennis and football, it does so without subjecting the joints to the impact of your body weight, or risking twists, tears or sprains. A study in 2016 found that cycling significantly reduced pain in arthritis sufferers by strengthening the surrounding muscle and boosting blood flow, which improved joint function.[3]

This is the case only if your riding position is correct, however. When pedalling, make sure your legs don't flare out at the top of the stroke. This is when most power is applied, and if your knees are splayed, that power will put your knee and ankle joints under strain. Watch your knees while you ride: they should appear to move up and down, but not in and out. If they do so, raise your saddle.

Change your body for the better

We've seen how cycling exercises the muscles and joints, keeping them healthy, but it doesn't stop there. Riding regularly – even as little as a 20-minute daily commute – will change your body in several other ways, all of them good for you.

Cardiovascular benefits

When your pulse increases, it strengthens your heart and improves circulation. With regular, vigorous riding (40 minutes, three or four times a week) you can also reduce your blood pressure and levels of low-density lipoproteins (the so-called bad cholesterol).

Chronic pain alleviation

A University of Michigan study in 2011 confirmed what doctors had suspected for many years: that regular exercise relieves long-term pain.[4] If you suffer from a bad back, for instance, regular bike riding may well be as effective as prescription painkillers.

Fat reduction

Any form of aerobic exercise will burn off fat, and cycling is no exception. As your muscles consume energy, they will (after about 30 minutes of exertion) start to deplete the fat reserves around your body – so cycling will, for instance, take weight off your belly, even though it's not working out those muscles. This has huge health benefits, including a decreased risk of diabetes, heart disease and cancer.

Balance and coordination improvements

As we get older, our sense of balance may become weaker. Riding a bike exercises the cerebellum, the part of the brain that coordinates our senses and muscles, and in particular is responsible for the tiny steering movements that keep a bike balanced – and account for its distinctive undulating tracks.

Bones
Surprisingly, given its other benefits, cycling does **not** promote strong bones. In 2012 a study found that racing cyclists who train for hours every day in fact run the risk of lowering their bone density.[5] But this isn't a risk for commuting or leisure cyclists, and it can be mitigated by regular off-bike exercise.

Ride more, boost your immunity

Your blood contains antibodies called immunoglobulins, which are produced by your white blood cells. They play a critical role in fighting off infection by recognizing and binding themselves to foreign invaders, such as bacteria or viruses.

Many studies have demonstrated a clear link between moderate exercise and immunoglobulin levels: exercise, especially regular exercise, boosts them, making you more resistant to disease and infection.[6] Also found in greater number in the blood of regular cyclists are several kinds of antibacterial, antiviral and cancer-fighting white blood cell, including neutrophils, NK (natural killer) cells, cytotoxic T cells and immature B cells. Many of these are made in the thymus, a tiny organ next to the heart, which is more active in older cyclists than in older non-cyclists.[7]

Exercise also boosts cytokines, anti-inflammatory proteins similar to hormones, which also reduce chronic inflammation in the body, in turn reducing harmful cortisol in the long term.

This all gives your immune system a powerful boost, helping you to fight off coughs, colds, flus and bacterial infections.

Age better

While improved resistance adds up to better health in the short term, what about the long haul?

Cycling makes a massive difference to your chances of a long and healthy life. A huge research project by the University of Glasgow compared the health of cycle commuters to the general population, finding that their mortality rates were lower for cancer (by 40 per cent), heart disease (by 42 per cent) and everything else to boot (by 41 per cent).[8] Because these figures take into account the (tiny) number of cyclists who die in accidents, they are an effective rejoinder to those who claim that the risks of cycling outweigh the health benefits.

Regular cyclists tend not to be overweight, which in turn reduces the risk of developing type 2 diabetes, a debilitating condition with serious consequences for your quality of life. The same applies with strokes.

Of course, a long life is much more enjoyable if your brain is in peak condition. A study by academics from University College London found that people over 50 who cycled (or e-biked) regularly had better cognitive function and mental health in general.[9] Exercise in midlife is a great way to keep your brain healthy: one 2009 review of multiple studies in this area found that the subjects who exercised the most cut their chances of developing dementia by 28 per cent, Parkinson's by 18 per cent, and Alzheimer's by a whopping 45 per cent.[10]

Want to live longer? Ride more.

Cycle yourself smarter

We've discovered how cycling makes us happier and fitter, but it brings another benefit too. When you ride, you exercise your brain, becoming smarter and, if you're commuting to work, better at your job.

One good reason to wear a helmet

Cycling works out our brains in a number of different ways – neurologically speaking, the areas highlighted opposite – including the instinctive, the cognitive and the emotional. That's all the more reason to protect it from bumps.

1

Frontal lobes

This part of the brain is where we do our conscious thinking and planning, so on the bike, it's where you plan your route and make decisions about why to go where. What's really interesting about the frontal lobes is that their performance is boosted by exercise. One study found that after a 30-minute ride, there are measurable improvements in cognition, particularly memory, reasoning and planning – all functions of this part of the brain.[11] Participants not only thought better, but also thought more quickly.

2

Motor cortex

This controls our voluntary movements: steering, pedalling and so on.

3

Cerebellum

This manages balance and coordinates our voluntary movements (from the motor cortex) with other sensory inputs, so we don't fall over. It's also important for learning motor behaviours, such as riding.

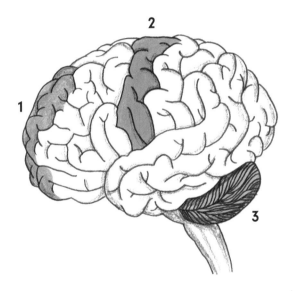

Hippocampus

Buried right in the centre of the brain, the hippocampus is the location of our mental maps. If you cycle widely around your city or town, learning numerous routes and locations, it will grow.

Hypothalamus

Located in the forebrain, the hypothalamus is not directly concerned with controlling the bike, but it does control the release of several hormones, including dopamine, one of the reasons we enjoy cycling so much.

The clever commuter

We power our bikes with our legs, but we ride them with our brains, and that gives our brains the kind of boost that we can use at work.

First, as we've already seen, cycling reduces stress by stimulating the release of hormones such as dopamine and anandamide, the so-called bliss molecule. We work better and focus more effectively when we are relaxed. Similarly, psychologists know that norepinephrine improves your mood and helps you to concentrate. This becomes a virtuous circle, since completing small accomplishments itself triggers the release of more norepinephrine – leading to the proverbial 'good day at the office'.

Increased blood flow and neural activity in the brain also bring benefits. As the circulation of oxygen to your brain (which needs more of it than any other organ) improves, so your powers of concentration, memory and analysis get stronger. At the same time, the neurons that fire as you ride *triple* the production of a protein called BDNF, which promotes the formation of new brain cells, keeps old ones healthy and reinforces long-term memory.

So if you want to think better, remember more and get more done, the answer is simple: ride your bike to work.

Going with the flow

Riding our bikes, especially in a slightly challenging situation such as going over rough terrain or through traffic, works out our brains, but doesn't stress them out. Instead, it brings us into the incredible mental state that psychologists call 'flow'.

Flow happens when our minds are busy, but not overtaxed: when you take on a challenge for which you have the necessary skill, yet which demands your full attention and concentration. This immersion in the present moment causes stress, anxiety and distraction to disappear, refreshing the brain and mind and leaving it energized and able to work more effectively at other times. You also lose track of time, feel less self-conscious, and find the ride enjoyable for its own sake. This means that your commute will not only feel quicker, but also be fun.

Flow is one of our greatest pleasures, the enjoyable element in any activity that absorbs you completely. If you have ever lost track of time when doing crossword puzzles, painting, gardening, woodwork or playing the piano, you will be familiar with the bliss that is flow, and its benefits. It is also a highly desirable state for anyone who thinks creatively for work or pleasure. As the keen city cyclist David Byrne explains in *The Bicycle Diaries* (2009):

> *It facilitates a state of mind that allows some but not too much of the unconscious to bubble up ... in the same way that perplexing problems sometimes get resolved in one's sleep, when the conscious mind is distracted the unconscious works things out.*

With one Oscar, a couple of Grammies, two bestselling books and the Talking Heads discography to his name, Byrne should know what he's talking about.

Another creative high achiever who used his bike to solve knotty problems was Albert Einstein. A keen cyclist and cyclo-tourist, Einstein deliberately sought flow through regular exercise, with spectacular results. When asked about his theory of general relativity, $E = mc^2$, he is reported to have said: 'I thought of that while riding my bicycle.'*

The lesson is clear: if you're tortured by a thorny question, you should put your pencil down, close the laptop, switch off the phone and go for a ride.

* It's unclear when, exactly, Einstein might have said these oft-quoted words; but he did more than once refer to an 'aha' moment that he had while riding one night, looking at the beam of his bicycle's lamp and realizing that the light it emitted came out at the same speed regardless of how fast the lamp itself was moving.

'I thought of that while riding my bicycle.'

Ride for your planet – and your home town

In the preceding pages we've looked at the good that cycling will do you, and seen that it makes for healthier, happier and smarter individuals. But when you ride you also make an impact on the place where you live, and the planet we all share. You may be surprised by how positive this impact is.

Your low-carbon machine

It's critical for us all to minimize our carbon footprints, and your bike helps to accomplish this in three ways. First, it consumes comparatively little material and energy, and therefore creates fewer emissions, when it's made. One estimate[12] is that manufacturing a typical bike results in CO_2 emissions of about 240 kg – which sounds a lot until you compare it to a MacBook laptop (264 kg) or a kilo of beef (about 300 kg of CO_2-equivalent emissions). Making a typical mid-sized car, meanwhile, results in emissions of about 17,000 kg – roughly speaking, 71 bicycles' worth.

Second, the bike emits very little carbon in use. If your regular rides are under an hour, you – the engine – are unlikely to demand extra calories for them, so the environmental impact is nil. A typical car, though, will burn through 5.6 litres of petrol every 100 km, and far

Manufacturing emissions of 1 car = 71 bikes

more in traffic. If you cycle that distance each week (as you will if you commute 10 km, or about 45 minutes, each way), then you undercut the car's emissions by about 13 kg of CO_2 every single week. If we put that into a global ecological context, every four or five weeks you alone are saving as much in emissions as one mature tree absorbs in a year.

Finally, you don't wear out the road surface the way a car or truck does. Road builders make complicated calculations based on traffic levels to predict when a road will need resurfacing, but they assume that bicycles are so light as to have zero impact. Since making new tarmac generates 33 times its weight in emissions, that's a huge environmental upside.

Given what we know about the dangers and costs of global heating, it's clear that widespread cycling *has* to be a significant part of the solution. And you can easily do your bit.

A cleaner, healthier city

A city with fewer cars is quieter and safer, especially for children. Its air will be cleaner; not only will carbon monoxide, nitrogen dioxide and other poisonous gases be at lower levels, but so will particulates, the tiny bits of grit that are also terrible for our cardiovascular health. A city with clean air will enjoy lower levels of stroke, heart disease, lung disease and asthma – all killers, and also expensive to treat.

By creating cities and towns where cycling is easy, quick and safe, we will also create a more active population. One benefit will be a reduced incidence of type 2 diabetes, a largely avoidable condition that is not only debilitating for sufferers but also hugely expensive for the taxpayer: over 10 per cent of the UK's national health budget goes on treating it and related conditions. If we all rode our bikes through adulthood, far fewer of us would develop it, and the money saved on healthcare could go towards happier things.

Living longer, with a higher quality of life, and spending less tax on unnecessary care: an inviting prospect, right?

The cycle-friendly environment

When you start to ride, environmental benefits are both the most and least important factor. They are the most important because they directly affect our world; and they are the least important because only a tiny number (some estimate just 1 per cent) of urban cyclists choose to ride for green reasons. The vast majority of us do it because it's the fastest way to get about.

So if we want to enjoy the environmental upside of a cycle-friendly city, we have to make it quick and safe to ride bikes – which means building dependable, wide, fast bike lanes on the direct routes that people actually need. Cycling itself is completely safe; it's motor traffic that is the source of danger, and we have to be prepared to take street space away from cars to make cyclists safe, cycling convenient, and our cities cleaner.

Many other efficiency benefits flow from a cycle-friendly city. One example: as online business grows,

home parcel delivery is becoming a crucial part of our infrastructure. Studies from Delhi, Singapore, Antwerp and elsewhere confirm that in cities, cargo bikes are a more efficient, timely way to deliver parcels and packages than vans, so your online order will not only have a lower carbon footprint, it'll also arrive that much more quickly.[13]

A bikeable city is a likeable city

For many years, urban cyclists around the world pointed to Amsterdam and Copenhagen as the world's best cycling cities – to the point that 'Copenhagenize' is now a verb used by town planners. While both remain, by the standards of most British or American cities, bike heaven, other cities around the world have been catching up fast. Munich now has a web of high-speed bike routes running into the city centre; Vancouver has systematically grown a similar network; Vienna has 1,400 km of bike lanes … and so on.

What else do these cities have in common? They are ranked among the very best places in the world to live, according to the annual Mercer index. Civic leadership in these places (and in a host of others around the world, from Bogotá to Taipei, and Utrecht to Auckland) recognizes that bike lanes are the fast track to a happier, safer, cleaner, healthier, more prosperous city – one where people want to live and work, and where they enjoy a higher quality of life.

How to Copenhagenize

Since the turn of the millennium Copenhagen has transformed the way its residents travel, and cycle journeys now outnumber car journeys there. Here's how they do it:

Count the people who travel, not the cars

For decades, planners tried to get cars, not human beings, to flow through cities: they counted vehicles, not people. As a result, our public space prioritizes car traffic, and pedestrians, cyclists and buses are expected to make way. By counting people instead, we see what the whole city needs – not just its motorists.

Share the space

The vast majority of available road space is given over to car traffic, even though car drivers are a minority of travellers. Slice space from car lanes and parking, and give it to cycle and bus lanes instead.

Give cyclists the straight lines they need

Direct routes across a town, connecting the places where people need to be, encourage them to ride. Let cyclists travel without detours, and they will grow in number.

Count the benefits

Cycling boosts the economy, our health and our businesses: add these benefits up. In Copenhagen they calculate that every kilometre cycled benefits society by 58 pence; every kilometre driven costs it 65 pence.

The amazing electric bike

The electric bike is already playing a huge part in the growth of cycling both for commuting and pleasure, and it looks as though it will only become more important. After an initial period in which governments struggled to classify e-bikes, the rules are now clear and easy to live with: in the UK, 'pedelec'-type bikes (in which the motor works only when the rider is pedalling) can use bike lanes, and require no registration or licence. These 'electrically assisted pedal cycles' are limited to 25 km/h, which is enough for a fast commute, and power output is limited to 250 watts – not quite what a Tour de France racer will produce, but significantly more than a normal human can.

You can easily spot an e-bike rider: they whizz along, turning their pedals suspiciously slowly while breathing through their nose. E-bikes take a lot of the effort out of a ride, making them less useful for athletes in training, but attractive for the rest of us, particularly if we live in windy or hilly places where riding has its painful moments.

Prices are coming down all the time as battery technology improves, and sales are booming. In the Netherlands, for instance, more than 40 per cent of all bike sales are e-bikes, and in the UK sales have been growing by around 50 per cent a year for several years. You can now get folding e-bikes and even high-end mountain e-bikes, so there will always be a model for you.

This stupendous sales growth is being driven by strong demand from riders who like what the e-bike has to offer. The advantages are numerous: you can load them more heavily than a conventional bike, you will be able to cycle for longer, so can travel further afield, you can commute faster (unless you're already pretty fit), and you don't have to be afraid of hills or headwinds any more.

From an urban planning point of view, they are a dream too. Not only do they use existing cycle infrastructure, but their greater range opens up longer commutes, which is especially valuable in large, sprawling cities such as London and New York. In the Netherlands, people are already taking full advantage of this; the average e-bike commuter rides 50 per cent further to work than a regular cycle commuter does. And, of course, pollution is zero, emissions from charging are low, and road surface wear is nil.

But isn't this all ... cheating? With 250 watts of electric motor picking up the strain, you'd imagine that e-bike riders use less energy, and therefore derive less exercise from cycling, than people on normal bikes. Paradoxically, the reverse is true. A study has found that because e-bike riders tend to make more, and longer, journeys, they actually burn up around 10 per cent *more* calories on their rides each week.[14]

Nearly all the health benefits – physical and mental – that accrue from regular cycling also come from e-cycling, and it seems as though many people who would otherwise be too nervous to ride are confident enough to try an electrically assisted bike. These include a significant number of older riders, and doctors now use e-bikes in cardiac rehabilitation programmes because they are suitable for gentle, easily controlled cardiovascular exercise.

The downsides? Weight is one; the battery and motor together may double the weight of your bike, and e-bikes typically tip the scales at 20 kg. This means that if you do happen to run out of juice, you've got a tiring ride home ahead of you. Battery life is another. Although this is improving all the time, it is likely that you will have to replace your battery after a few years, and treat it carefully in the meantime. Protect it from extreme heat or cold when charging, charge it up when it's between 30 and 60 per cent of capacity, don't leave it plugged in to charge for long periods, and don't leave it uncharged for long periods.

The cycling community

'Infrastructure' is a long word with boring connotations, but it refers to a host of things that we find useful, fun, or both. A town with a strong cycling infrastructure will encourage cyclists to come together, strengthening the community and bringing yet more benefits.

Docking stations and secure bike parks at railway and bus stations deter thieves and encourage drivers to leave their vehicle at home and ride in instead. Well-designed bike lanes make it safer and quicker to commute, and encourage less confident riders, children and the old. Local bike shops run by passionate mechanics (much better than chain stores with unqualified staff) are a free source of advice and expertise, and can often connect you with a local club or tell you about good local routes. Club rides are a great way to build your fitness and, if you're the competitive type, pit yourself against others.

Best of all – if you are lucky enough to have one in your town – is a community bike workshop, which will help you to fix your machine and get to know it better than ever. These places often do many other good things: distributing free bikes to refugees, running cycle training for schools, and so on. If you are near one, support it.

There is an invisible thread that connects cyclists to coffee and cake, and most cities now have a few cafés that are either explicitly dedicated to bikes, or are the unofficial base for local group rides. These too are a good source of fellowship, knowledge and practical help.

None of this infrastructure, which makes our lives so much better, emerges from thin air. Businesses need your support, so spend your money with them. The local politicians and planners who are ultimately responsible for the creation of a cycle-friendly city, with all the good things that follow, need your input. Vote for cycle-friendly candidates, sign petitions, join local groups, comment on planning applications and in general do everything you can to let them know that you – that we – exist.

PART FOUR

Further Afield

Now that you're up and running, and
enjoying the financial, mental, emotional
and physical benefits of everyday cycling, you
can start thinking about riding further for fun.
Touring, for a day or longer, is a fantastic
way to enjoy countryside and coastlines
and discover new horizons.

Route planning

If time is no object, cycling without a map is a great way to get to know a large city. Point yourself roughly where you need to go, follow your nose and see where it leads you. Going off the main roads, you'll encounter less traffic and unearth all kinds of shortcuts, surprising corners and new neighbourhoods.

Of course, the 'detour ride' is nothing new – cyclists have been 'taking the longest route possible to stretch out the fun', as the writer Lady Vélo puts it, since bikes were invented. Sure, you might ride a little further than you absolutely need to, but it's worth it for the experience.

The advent of smartphones with GPS location-finding and Google maps gives exploring another dimension. Now, before you leave, you can set a course that steers you through a new corner of the city, and just follow your phone's directions.

Many cities all over the world have rapidly rethought their cycle networks as a response to Covid-19. Many roads that would once have been busy with motor vehicles are now quiet; others have suddenly acquired wide cycle lanes. Councils have seized the moment to block off some routes to motor traffic, creating newly quiet bike-friendly routes. Now is a good time to investigate new options.

Off-road, though, Google and its competitors are unreliable. In the UK, the Ordnance Survey's excellent

Explorer maps clearly identify which paths are legal to ride on and which aren't, and if you don't fancy wrestling with an oversized map sheet at the roadside, you can download a digital copy to your phone.

If you want to measure your performance – and work out how many calories you've burned off – Strava, a tracking app for runners and riders, is a brilliant solution, and free to download. As well as measuring your speed, it will save your route on a map, tell you the vertical distance you've climbed, and more. Serious racers use Garmin, which unites navigation and performance tracking in a purpose-built handlebar computer; this is more expensive, but popular.

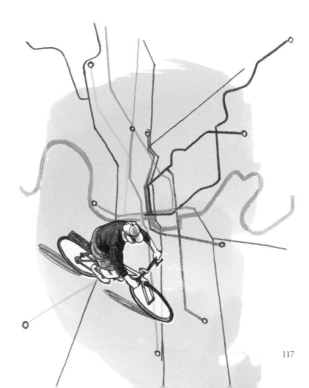

Touring

Once you've fallen for cycling, you may well feel the urge to take a break on two wheels. The world is full of beautiful countryside with quiet lanes and pathways, and touring by bike is one of the best ways to enjoy it.

You go at your own pace, easily carrying enough gear to camp comfortably, and being completely mobile makes it simple to find a good spot to rest, eat or admire the view. You should service your bike first, and a rack and large waterproof panniers are essential, but otherwise you don't need special equipment.

You'll find that a day in the open air, with gentle exercise and the stimulation of a steadily changing landscape, is amazingly relaxing. It's easy to meet the locals, and you don't have to worry about parking or any of the other downsides of driving. A day spent travelling in a car is stressful; a day spent pedalling through countryside, free to stop whenever you like and in control of your time, is bliss. And at the end of it, you even come back fitter than when you left.

Everyone tours their own way, but here are some ideas to work into your next summer holiday or long weekend.

Credit card

Despite its name, credit-card touring isn't an exclusive pastime for the rich. It's when you deliberately travel light – packing just a couple of changes of clothes and emergency waterproofs – and ride between B&Bs or hotels. With lighter bags, and warm showers, hot meals and comfortable beds waiting at the end of each day, this is definitely a comfortable option.

Station to station

If time is short, you may not be able to get away from home for a long tour, and you'll find that regular rides will exhaust local possibilities pretty quickly. Station-to-station rides are an excellent way to expand your range. Take the train to somewhere new, then ride home, or to another station. An hour or so's train journey out will give you a leisurely ride home for the rest of the day, and show you some new country.

Fully loaded

With a full set of panniers, and probably a rack bag and a bar bag too, the fully loaded tourist carries everything they need from day to day: tent, stove, food, sleeping bag, mat and all. This gives you total flexibility and is also (once you've bought all the kit) cheap; all you need to pay for is food. You may miss the creature comforts, and have to wash using the same pan you cook in, but it's incredibly liberating.

Expeditionary

This is like the 'fully loaded' option described opposite, but with some kind of challenging goal in mind: a round-the-world, coast-to-coast, months-long, life-changing adventure. There could be a book deal in it, too, if things go dramatically wrong.

Transcontinental

One of Europe's little-known glories, the EuroVelo network is a collection of 17 cycle-friendly routes that link every country on the Continent. Why not pick one of these for the ride of a lifetime? EuroVelo 11, the East Europe Route, for instance, runs all the way from northern Norway to Athens in Greece – 11 countries, 6 capital cities and 6,550 kilometres – taking in beautiful countryside all the way. If that's a little ambitious for you, there are less challenging rides down the Rhine, Rhône, Elbe or Danube rivers, or coastal routes everywhere from Scotland to Cyprus.

In the United States, the TransAmerica Trail offers an equally varied experience, running from Oregon to Virginia and taking in the Grand Teton National Park, Yellowstone National Park and other spectacular locations. Because the same route has been ridden since the mid-1970s, many of its cafés and places to stay have visitors' books full of entries from other riders – an amazing record of decades of cycling adventure.

Ride on!

Writing and researching this slim volume has been an eye-opening experience. The last book I wrote about cycle culture and the joys of riding came out in 2011, and the fresh scientific and medical research published since that time has transformed our understanding of the positive effects of bikes on our lives. Getting stuck into all this new knowledge has been fascinating, and it's a pleasure to share it.

We used to love cycling instinctively because it made us feel great; now we know how it does so. We used to have a vague sense that the working day went better if we commuted by bike; now we know it definitely does. We used to live in hope of our cities becoming more bike-friendly; now we see it happening (albeit frustratingly slowly) around us.

As a new cyclist, whether you've got on your bike because of Covid-19 or not, you are one among many millions, part of a generation that will not only be healthier as a result, but also contribute to everyone else's good health, and that of the planet. Keep at it – we need each other. Ride confidently, ride considerately, ride happily. Explore your home town and the countryside that surrounds it. Enjoy looking after your bike and being part of the community of cyclists. It is an amazing machine, and riding it is an amazing thing to do.

See you on the road.

Resources

Cycling UK (formerly known as the Cyclist's Touring Club) has a comprehensive register of local clubs and campaign groups, as well as great member benefits, including insurance, discounts, route plans and more: www.cyclinguk.org

Cycling Australia is more focused on competitive riding, but also offers insurance: www.cycling.org.au

In **New Zealand**, CAN (the Cycling Action Network) represents everyday cyclists: www.can.org.nz

Books
Richard Ballantine, *Richard's Bicycle Book*, 1972

David Byrne, *The Bicycle Diaries*, 2009

Ben Irvin, *Einstein and the Art of Mindful Cycling: Achieving Balance in the Modern World*, 2012

Nick Moore, *Mindful Thoughts for Cyclists: Finding Balance on Two Wheels*, 2017

Jools Walker (Lady Vélo), *Back in the Frame: How to Get Back on Your Bike, Whatever Life Throws at You*, 2018

References

1. Walker, I. and Robinson, D., 'Bicycle Helmet Wearing Is Associated with Closer Overtaking by Drivers: A Response to Olivier and Walter, 2013', *Accident Analysis and Prevention*, 123 (2019), pp. 107–13.

2. Samadi, Z., Taghian, F., and Valiani, M., 'The Effects of 8 Weeks of Regular Aerobic Exercise on the Symptoms of Premenstrual Syndrome in Non-athlete Girls', *Iranian Journal of Nursing and Midwifery Research*, 18/1 (2013), pp. 14–19.

3. Alkatan, M., Baker, J., et al., 'Improved Function and Reduced Pain after Swimming and Cycling Training in Patients with Osteoarthritis', *Journal of Rheumatology*, 43/3 (March 2016), pp. 666–72.

4. Hassett, A. and Williams, D., 'Non-pharmacological Treatment of Chronic Widespread Musculoskeletal Pain', *Best Practice and Research: Clinical Rheumatology*, 25/2 (April 2011), pp. 299–309.

5. Olmedillas, H., Gonzáles-Agüero, A., Moreno, L.A., et al., 'Cycling and Bone Health: A Systematic Review', *BMC Medicine*, 10/1 (2012), p. 168.

6. Nieman, D. and Wentz, L., 'The Compelling Link Between Physical Activity and the Body's Defense System', *Journal of Sport and Health Science*, 8/3 (May 2019), pp. 201–17.

7. Duggal, N.A., Pollock, R.D., et al., 'Major Features of Immune Senescence, Including Reduced Thymic Output, Are Ameliorated by High Levels of Physical Activity in Adulthood', *Aging Cell*, 17/2 (April 2018).

8. Celis-Morales, C., Lyall, D., Welsh, P., Anderson, J., Steel, L., Guo, Y., et al., 'Association Between Active Commuting and Incident Cardiovascular Disease, Cancer, and Mortality: Prospective Cohort Study', *British Medical Journal*, April 2017, p. 357.

9. Leyland, L.A., Spencer, B., et al., 'The Effect of Cycling on Cognitive Function and Well-being in Older Adults', *PLOS One*, 14/2 (2019).

10. Hamer, M. and Chida Y., 'Physical Activity and Risk of Neurodegenerative Disease: A Systematic Review of Prospective Evidence', *Psychological Medicine,* 39/1 (2009), pp. 3–11.

11. Nanda, B., Balde, J. and Manjunatha, S., 'The Acute Effects of a Single Bout of Moderate-intensity Aerobic Exercise on Cognitive Functions in Healthy Adult Males', *Journal of Clinical Diagnostic Research*, 7/9 (September 2013), pp. 1883–5.

12. Dave, S., 'Life Cycle Assessment of Transportation Options for Commuters', Master's thesis presented to Massachusetts Institute of Technology (MIT) February 2010 https://files.meetup.com/1468133/LCAwhitepaper.pdf

13. Dalla Chiara, G., Alho, A.R., et al., 'Exploring Benefits of Cargo-cycles versus Trucks for Urban Parcel Delivery under Different Demand Scenarios', *Transportation Research Record*, 2674/5 (May 2020), pp. 553–62.

14. Castro, A., 'Physical Activity of Electric Bicycle Users Compared to Conventional Bicycle Users and Non-cyclists: Insights Based on Health and Transport Data from an Online Survey in Seven European Cities', *Transportation Research Interdisciplinary Perspectives*, 1 (June 2019).

Acknowledgements

At an impressionable age I came across, and devoured, my father's copy of *Richard's Bicycle Book* by Richard Ballantine, and I still think of it most times I ride – which means nearly every day. It opened my mind. From then on, cycling was not just convenient, cheap, fun and healthy, it was a thought-provoking, philosophical activity, and one way to make a better world. Ballantine was an inspiring advocate of the personal and social benefits of cycling, and this volume owes his plenty, including the quotation on page 86.

My thanks go to Zara Larcombe, who conceived this book; Melissa Mellor, who calmly managed its progress; Rosie Fairhead, who edited the manuscript; and Trish Burgess, who proofread the layouts. Any mistakes are mine, not theirs. Having admired his work for years, I am delighted to appear in print with the illustrator David Sparshott: the designer Alex Coco made his work, and mine, look fantastic on the page. Thanks also to the rest of the amazing team at Laurence King Publishing – including Barney, Fiona, Marc, Laurence, Adrian, Angus, Felicity, everyone at ACBUK, and their international colleagues at Chronicle Books, BIS and LKP Verlag.

I am hugely grateful for the freely shared knowledge and community spirit of the people of Cranks in Brighton. Finally, I am lucky to live with Jules Hau, Sid Allen and LB de la Mer, the best roomies any author could hope for.

ALAN ANDERSON grew up cycling around London, back when bike lanes were scarce, the pollution was disgusting and everything on wheels got stolen, all the time. Undeterred, he carried on riding everywhere, has written three books about bicycles and cycle culture, and volunteers at a community bike workshop near his home.

DAVID SPARSHOTT is a graduate of Bristol School of Art and Design and has worked as a freelance illustrator for over a decade. A true cycling fan, he enjoys the simple pleasures of a solo ride in the Suffolk countryside as much as the elaborate aesthetics of the professional peloton.